They use them to trap their **prey** on the ocean floor.

Body

Some hammerhead sharks are greenish in color. Others are gray.

Table of Contents

Hammerhead Sharks

Hammerhead sharks
have wide and flat heads.
They look like hammers.

This is how hammerhead sharks got their name.

Their wide heads
make them good hunters.

All hammerhead sharks
have white bellies.

Hammerhead sharks
have large **dorsal fins**.

Their eyes are on the sides of their heads. This helps them see a wide area. They can find prey easily.

Habitat

Hammerhead sharks live in warm ocean water. You can often find them near coasts.

Zoom In on Sharks

Hammerhead Sharks

Leo Statts

abdopublishing.com

Published by Abdo Zoom™, PO Box 398166, Minneapolis, Minnesota 55439. Copyright © 2018 by Abdo Consulting Group, Inc. International copyrights reserved in all countries. No part of this book may be reproduced in any form without written permission from the publisher. Abdo Zoom™ is a trademark and logo of Abdo Consulting Group, Inc.

Printed in the United States of America, North Mankato, Minnesota
042017
092017

Cover Photo: Shutterstock Images
Interior Photos: Shutterstock Images, 1, 5, 8, 10, 12–13, 14; Grant M. Henderson/Shutterstock Images, 4–5; Tomas Kotouc/Shutterstock Images, 6; Joost van Uffelen/Shutterstock Images, 7; Denis Korneev/Shutterstock Images, 9; iStockphoto, 11, 15; Red Line Editorial, 13, 20 (left), 20 (right), 21 (left), 21 (right); Bernd Neeser/Shutterstock Images, 16; Yann Hubert/Shutterstock Images, 17; Marion Kraschl/Shutterstock Images, 18–19

Editor: Emily Temple
Series Designer: Madeline Berger
Art Direction: Dorothy Toth

Publisher's Cataloging-in-Publication Data
Names: Statts, Leo, author.
Title: Hammerhead sharks / by Leo Statts.
Description: Minneapolis, MN : Abdo Zoom, 2018. | Series: Sharks |
    Includes bibliographical references and index.
Identifiers: LCCN 2017931667 | ISBN 9781532120091 (lib. bdg.) |
    ISBN 9781614797203 (ebook) | 9781614797760 (Read-to-me ebook)
Subjects: LCSH: Hammerhead sharks--Juvenile literature. | Sharks--Juvenile
    literature.
Classification: DDC 597.3/4--dc23
LC record available at http://lccn.loc.gov/2017931667

They have **sensors** in their heads. These sense movement. This helps the sharks find prey.

Hammerhead sharks eat fish.

They also eat stingray or octopus. They even eat other sharks.

Hammerhead **pups** have rounded heads. Their heads become flat as they grow.

Hammerhead sharks live up to 30 years in the wild.

Shortest Length

A scalloped bonnethead shark is shorter than an acoustic guitar.

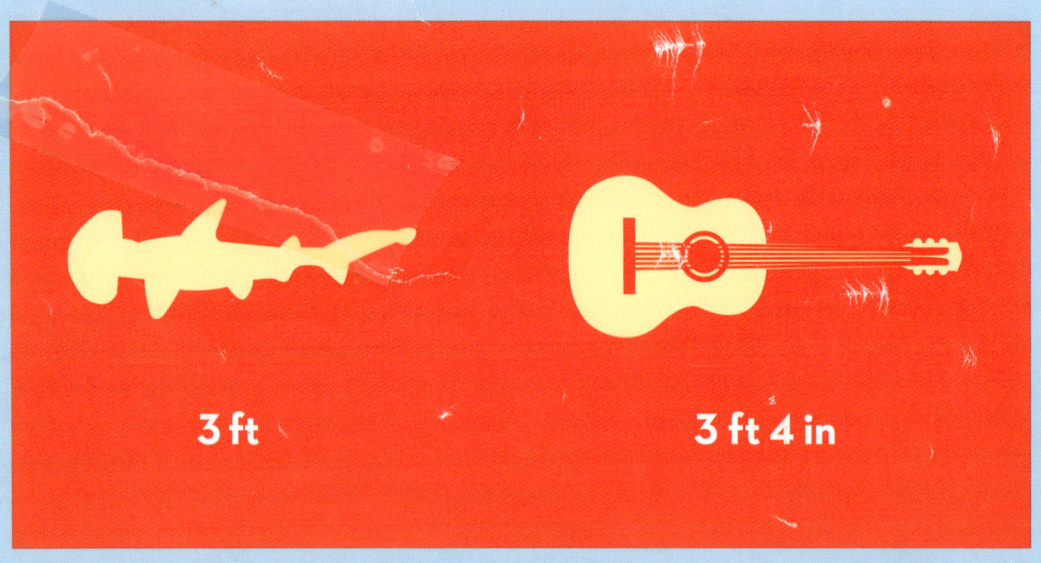

3 ft   3 ft 4 in

Longest Length

A great hammerhead is longer than a car.

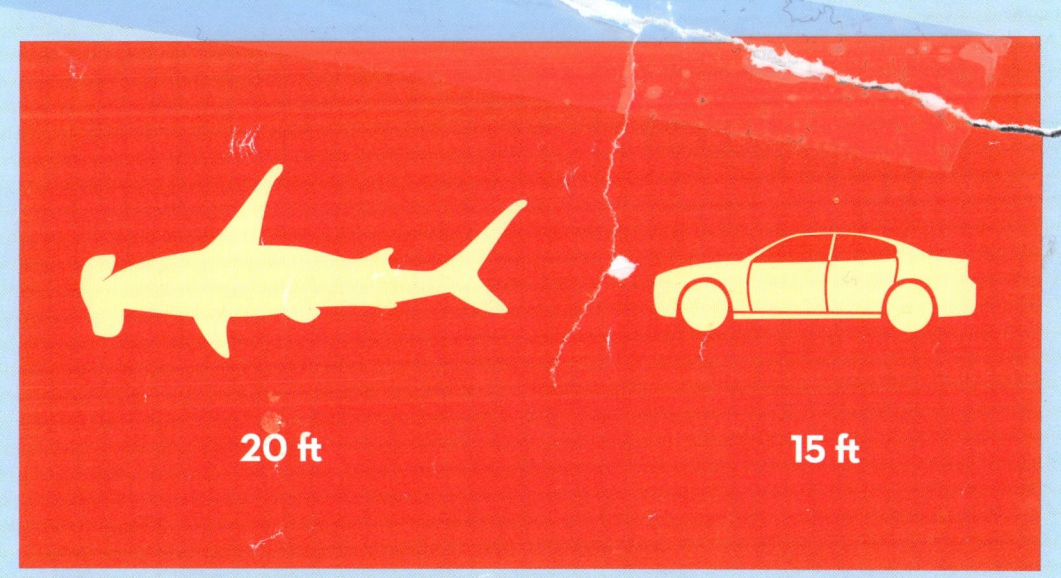

Glossary

coast - where land and water meet.

dorsal fin - the tall, triangular fin on a sea animal's back.

predator - an animal that hunts other animals.

prey - an animal hunted for food.

pup - a newborn shark.

sensor - a special body part that can detect nearby objects.

Booklinks

For more information on **hammerhead sharks**, please visit abdobooklinks.com

Zoom In on Animals!

Learn even more with the Abdo Zoom Animals database. Check out **abdozoom.com** for more information.

Index

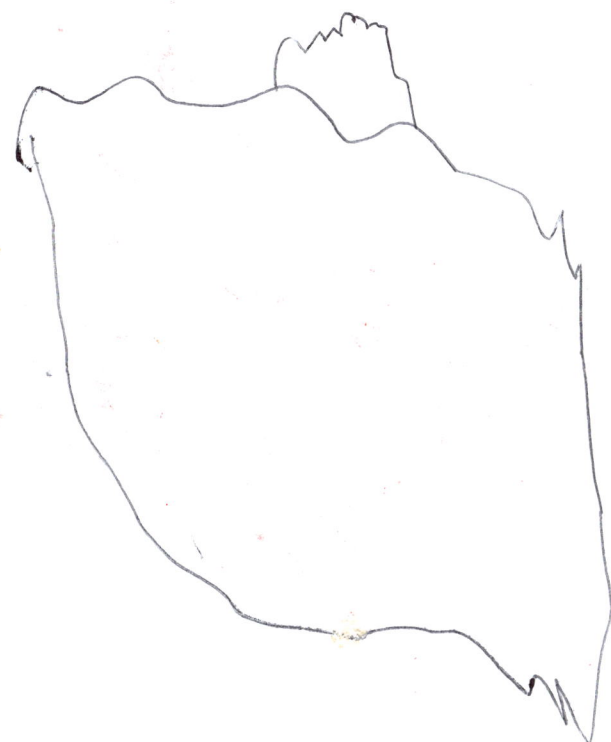